D0971187

OTHER BOOKS IN THIS SERIES:
Thank Heavens for Friends   To my Grandmother with Love
For Mother, a Gift of Love   Marriage a Keepsake
Love a Celebration   For My Father
Words of Comfort

EDITED BY HELEN EXLEY
BORDER ILLUSTRATIONS BY SHARON BASSIN

Published simultaneously in 1994 by Helen Exley Giftbooks
in Great Britain, and Helen Exley Giftbooks LLC in the USA.

12 11 10 9 8

Picture and text selection by © Helen Exley 1994.
Border Illustrations © Sharon Bassin 1994.
The moral right of the author has been asserted.

ISBN 1-85015-895-9

Picture research by Image Select International.
Text research by Margaret Montgomery.
Typeset by Delta, Watford.
Printed and bound in China.

Helen Exley Giftbooks 16 Chalk Hill, Watford,
Herts WD1 4BN, United Kingdom.
Helen Exley Giftbooks LLC, 185 Main Street,
Spencer, MA 01562, USA.

To my
DAUGHTER
with love

A Helen Exley Giftbook

EXLEY
NEW YORK • WATFORD, UK

[Welcoming a newborn baby is] somehow absolute, truer and more binding than any other experience life has to offer.

MARILYN FRENCH

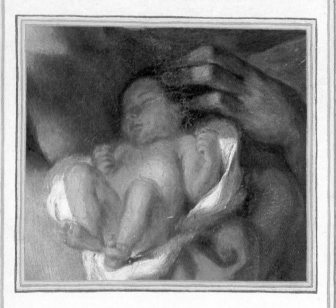

YOU BEING BORN

But for those moments, as the doctor
shoved cotton wool up your flat nose
and swabbed your eyes and cleaned your bum
I forgot completely all my life and love
and watched you like a pool of growing light
and whispered to myself "She's come!
    She's come!"

BRIAN JONES

Then someone placed her in my arms. She
looked up at me. The crying stopped. Her eyes
melted through me, forging a connection in me
with their soft heat.

SHIRLEY MACLAINE

Romance fails us – and so do friendships – but
the relationship – of Mother and Child –
remains indelible and indestructible – the
strongest bond upon this earth.

THEODOR REIK

From the instant I saw her, a tiny red creature bathed in the weird underwater light of the hospital operating room, I loved her with an intensity that life had not prepared me for.

Susan Cheever

Here she was then, my daughter, here alive, the one I must possess and guard. A year before this space had been empty, not even a hope of her was in it. Now she was here, brand new, with our name upon her, and no one could call in the night to reclaim her.

She was here for good, her life stretching before us, and so new I couldn't leave her alone.

Laurie Lee, from "Two Women"

Dad has long and earnest conversations with his baby daughter. He tells her she is noisy, undisciplined and manipulative – and she will be sent back if she doesn't pull herself together. And the baby smiles complacently.
She has him exactly where she wants him.

Pam Brown

When you came into the world I suffered for three days and two nights. But I have never regarded that as suffering.

They say that children like you who have been carried so high in the womb and have taken so long to come down to the daylight are always the children that are most loved, because they have lain so near the mother's heart and have been so unwilling to leave her.

Sidonie Goudeket, to her daughter, Colette

So why didn't I feel resentful, sitting here day after day, pumping away ... 2oz, 3oz ... milk which the baby would probably reject when offered to her in a bottle as extra pudding after her feed? I suppose the answer was, I had discovered true love. The love which repays slavery and exhaustion with a brief smile. But what a smile! It was more than enough. My present prostration was somehow sweeter than all the pleasures of my past life.

Sue Limb, from "Love Forty"

I was continually amazed by the way in which I could watch for hours nothing but the small movements of her hands, and the fleeting expressions of her face. She was a very happy child, and once she learned to smile, she never stopped; at first she would smile at anything, at parking meters and dogs and strangers, but as she grew older she began to favour me, and nothing gave me more delight than her evident preference. I suppose I had not really expected her to dislike and resent me from birth, though I was quite prepared for resentment to follow later on, but I certainly had not anticipated such wreathing, dazzling gaiety of affection from her whenever I happened to catch her eye. Gradually I began to realize that she liked me, that she had no option to liking me, and that unless I took great pains to alienate her she would go on liking me, for a couple of years at least. It was very pleasant to receive such uncritical love, because it left me free to bestow love; my kisses were met by small warm rubbery unrejecting cheeks and soft dovey mumblings of delight.

MARGARET DRABBLE, FROM "THE MILLSTONE"

In the midst of this endless ordeal, this dark tunnel where I now lived, cut off from ordinary life, only dimly aware of the spring taking place as if it were on some remote planet; in the midst of it all, an extraordinary thing happened. I was feeding Beano one night, just before midnight, when she stopped, looked up at me, and suddenly broke into a delicious smile. "Van Dyke!" I cried. "She's smiling! Come quick! She's smiling at me!"

Van Dyke came, and to my amazement the baby turned her head to him and gave him a big smile, too. It was an extraordinary moment: something electric. It was as if somebody had just come into the room. Up till now, we'd admired her quiet alertness and her wakeful curiosity, but had received from her nothing but a rather stern stare. It was as if, all at once, she was a person at last: had joined us. This smile wreathed itself about my heart. It was the moment of a lifetime, never to be forgotten. I felt ravished by some divine spark of joy.

SUE LIMB, FROM "LOVE FORTY"

A Daughter. An astonishment. A perfection. The newest thing in the world. So small. So packed with secrets.

And every day brings fresh wonders – for every smile, every gesture is an enchantment. Everything is unexpected. (Quick! – see what she's doing now!)

Her face lights up when you – most ordinary you – come into sight. Your songs delight her. You are the one who can soothe her into sleep, drive off her terrors, lever her from tears to laughter.

She is so beautiful, so funny, so eager, so resolute.

And she loves you with all her heart.

No one has failed who has so dear a daughter.

PAM BROWN

...my darling girl
Sleeps and smiles and laughs, her face
So full of curiosity and magic
That I know the world was
Made in her honour.
She looks around her and as she looks
She renews all she sees.
The leaves rustle excitedly,
The curtains dance by the window,
The shadow moves beside her as
She turns and she turns and she turns,
Ocean eyes,
Taking it all in.

SALLY EMERSON, FROM "BACK TO WORK"

Daughters are a delight.
Some of the time. Most of the time.
When, that is, they are not putting their white ballet tights into the wash inside black jeans; when they are not declaring there's not a *single* egg in the hen house when you've been averaging thirty a day; when they are not discovering they haven't *one* clean shirt – three minutes before the school bus leaves; when they are not sitting in front of the dictionary, vowing they can't find any word like aggravating. And that they *hate* tomato sandwiches and always *always* have done. Though they devoured an entire plateful at last week's party....

Daughters are a delight.

PAM BROWN

A little girl can be sweeter (and badder) oftener than anyone else in the world. She can jitter around, and stomp, and make funny noises that frazzle your nerves, yet just when you open your mouth she stands there demure with that special look in her eyes. A girl is Innocence playing in the mud. Beauty standing on its head, and Motherhood dragging a doll by the foot.

ALAN BECK

They have what no grown up has – that directness – chatter, chatter, chatter, on Ann goes, in a kind of world of her own, with its seals and dogs; happy because she's going to have cocoa tonight, and go blackberrying tomorrow.

The walls of her mind are all hung round with such bright vivid things, and she doesn't see what we see.

VIRGINIA WOOLF, FROM "A WRITER'S DIARY"

But I did kiss you in the night
and chased away your nightmares;
and I made up stories and songs
that made you laugh full and strong,
and most times, I was there for you
and recognized, most clearly
that facing you is facing me.

And I encouraged you to claim your life
and fight like hell for your right to be;
and the best gift that I could ever give to you
was to say "yes" to your dreams
that were not my own.

Margaret Sloan-Hunter, from "Passing"

A LITTLE
UNCOMPLICATED
HYMN

for Joy

is what I wanted to write.
There *was* such a song!

A song for your kneebones,
a song for your ribs,
those delicate trees that bury
    your heart;
a song for your bookshelf
where twenty hand-blown ducks
    sit in a Venetian row;
a song for your dress-up high
    heels,
your fire-red skate board
your twenty grubby fingers,
the pink knitting that you start
and never quite finish;
your poster-paint pictures,
all angels making a face,
a song for your laughter
that keeps wiggling a spoon
    in my sleep.

ANNE SEXTON

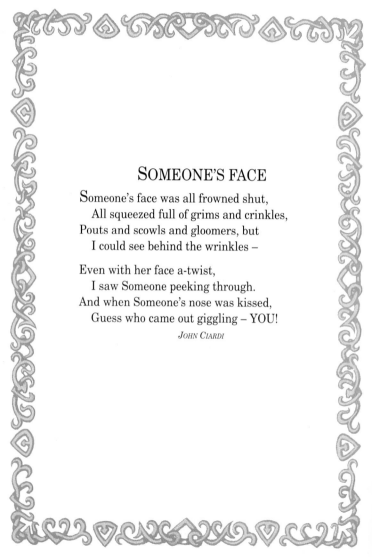

SOMEONE'S FACE

Someone's face was all frowned shut,
   All squeezed full of grims and crinkles,
Pouts and scowls and gloomers, but
   I could see behind the wrinkles –

Even with her face a-twist,
   I saw Someone peeking through.
And when Someone's nose was kissed,
   Guess who came out giggling – YOU!

JOHN CIARDI

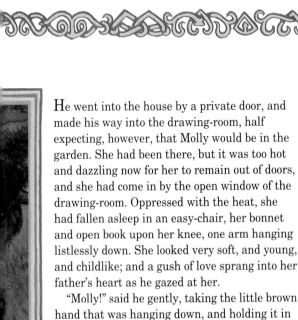

He went into the house by a private door, and made his way into the drawing-room, half expecting, however, that Molly would be in the garden. She had been there, but it was too hot and dazzling now for her to remain out of doors, and she had come in by the open window of the drawing-room. Oppressed with the heat, she had fallen asleep in an easy-chair, her bonnet and open book upon her knee, one arm hanging listlessly down. She looked very soft, and young, and childlike; and a gush of love sprang into her father's heart as he gazed at her.

"Molly!" said he gently, taking the little brown hand that was hanging down, and holding it in his own. "Molly!"

She opened her eyes, that for one moment had no recognition in them. Then the light came brilliantly into them and she sprang up, and threw her arms round his neck, exclaiming:

"Oh, papa, my dear, dear papa! What made you come while I was asleep? I lose the pleasure of watching for you."

Mrs. Gaskell, from "Wives and Daughters"

Little girls are the nicest things that happen to people. They are born with a little bit of angelshine about them, and though it wears thin sometimes there is always enough left to lasso your heart – even when they are sitting in the mud, or crying temperamental tears, or parading up the street in mother's best clothes.

ALAN BECK

What feeling is so nice as a child's hand in yours? So small, so soft and warm, like a kitten huddling in the shelter of your clasp.

MARJORIE HOLMES

LITTLE GIRL

I will buy you a house
If you do not cry,
A house, little girl,
As big as the sky.

I will build you a house
Of golden dates,
The freshest of all
For the steps and the gates.

I will furnish the house
For you and for me,
With walnuts and hazels
Fresh from the tree.

I will build you a house
And when it is done,
I will roof it with grapes
To keep out the sun.

ROSE FYLEMAN
(FROM AN ARABIAN NURSERY RHYME)

Daughter, take this amulet
tie it with cord and caring
I'll make you a chain of coral and pearl
to glow on your neck. I'll dress you nobly.
A gold clasp too – fine, without flaw
to keep with you always.
When you bathe, sprinkle perfume, and weave
    your hair in braids.
String jasmine for the counterpane,
Wear your clothes like a bride,
for your feet anklets, bracelets for your arms ...
Don't forget rosewater,
don't forget henna for the palms of your hands.

Mwana Kupona Msham, from "Poem To Her Daughter"

In giving our daughter life, her father and I had also given her death, something I hadn't realized until that new creature flailed her arms in what was now infinite space. We had given her disease and speeding cars and flying cornices: once out of the fortress that had been myself, she would never be safe again.... We disappoint our kids and they disappoint us, and sometimes they grow up into people we don't like very much. We go on loving, though what we love may be more memory than actuality. And until the day we die we fear the phone that rings in the middle of the night.

MARY CANTWELL

For my sake, pray cherish the person whom I love above all others in the world.

MME. DE SEVIGNE, IN A LETTER TO HER DAUGHTER

To me the only answer a woman can make to the destructive forces of the world is creation. And the most ecstatic form of creation is the creation of new life.

JESSIE BERNARD, TO HER UNBORN DAUGHTER

MY JEWEL

God keep my jewel this day from all danger;
From tinker and pooka and black-hearted
    stranger;
From harm of the water, and hurt of the fire;
From the horns of the cows going home from the
    byre;
From teasing the ass when he's tied to the
    manger;
From stones that would bruise and from thorns
    of the briar;
From evil red berries that waken desire;
From hunting the gander and vexing the goat;
From cut and from tumble, from sickness and
    weeping;
May God have my jewel this day in His keeping.

W.M. Letts

But as she'd grown as a daughter, so I'd grown as a father, and learnt to bury away my wishful images of her, and to watch her take charge, naturally enough, of her own directions and to develop her own independence and will.

So what I'd got now was not the compliant doll of a father's fancy, but a glowing girl with a dazzling and complicated personality, one with immense energy in chasing both happiness and despair, and who expressed her love for me, as always, not in secret half-smiles and the sharing of silences, but in noisy shouts, jolly punches, sharp jabs to the stomach, and a lively burying of teeth in arms and earlobes.

Certainly she had become no dad's soft shadow, nor ever would be now. She was existing on a different scale to my first fond imaginings. She had become herself – a normal jeans-clad, horse-riding, pop-swinging, guitar-bashing adolescent with a huge appetite for the lustier pleasures of life.

Not at all what I planned or what I expected, but I know I didn't wish her changed.

LAURIE LEE, FROM "TWO WOMEN"

The baby was born and your life was changed more than you ever dreamed. You found you had sprouted invisible antennae that picked up every alteration in breathing, every variation in temperature, every nuance of expression in your tiny daughter.

No one told you that the change was irreversible. That you would feel in your own heart every pain, every loss, every disappointment, every rebuff, every cruelty that she experiences – life long.

ROSANNE AMBROSE-BROWN, b.1943

A daughter is a cloud of talc, an oil ring round the bath, a sink drain full of hair, a strew of sodden towels.

A daughter is a pile of clothes – a mix of worn and clean. A tangle of tights. A heap of single shoes.

A daughter is a slam of doors. A crying in the bathroom. A heap of sulk.

A daughter is an abandoner of cups and plates and apple cores. A drift of chocolate wrappers. A cult of diets.

A daughter is car doors banging in the early hours.

A daughter is that tiny body that you carried home.

...Incredibly.

But still, inside, the same.

PAM BROWN

The teenage girl has won herself a reputation for intractability.... Yet there is another side to the story, not often told but experienced by many mothers. So I make no apology for singing a few glad tidings on the loving, happy aspects of the young western European girl growing into womanhood at the side of her mother.

They come mostly from the girl's freshness, her curiosity, her openness, her irresponsibility, her exuberance (despite all pressures), her affection, her loyalty, her sympathy, her gentleness, her wide-eyed enjoyment of things that her mother has started to take for granted or lost interest in altogether.

RACHEL BILLINGTON, FROM "THE GREAT UMBILICAL"

Dear Daughter.
You cost me a fortune in nappies
and gripe water, shoes and skirts
and hockey sticks. You broke my
sleep, you broke my golfing trophy
and you nearly broke my heart on
several occasions. You were
obstinate, noisy, rude, untidy,
argumentative, disobedient, lazy –
and you backed the car over my
geraniums. You read the wrong
books, studied the wrong subjects,
got the wrong qualifications.
Your boyfriends have been
near certifiable.
But you're wonderful.
And I love you.
Dad.

Dr. Peter Spears

The parent stares incredulously at this creature sprawled across the sofa, eating take-aways, semi-comatose and sustained by a cacophony of sound.

Will it, all parents wonder, ever complete the metamorphosis and become an adult human being?

Or will it lie there forever, smelling of Ysatis, vinegar and sweat?

At this point many mothers and fathers take on a strange, withdrawn look. They have given up. They have opted out. They are reviewing their finances to see if emigration is possible.

At this point, overnight there is a tearing noise, like the giving way of ancient, well-loved jeans.

And out of the teenage shell full-formed, amiable, conversational, hard-thinking, sane, steps a full-blown daughter.

And, after all, everyone *was* right.

It is wonderful to be a mother or father.

Dearest, dearest daughter, welcome to the Human Race!

PAM BROWN

TO TERI, LEAVING HOME

When the day comes for your child to leave home, you want them to be able to say, "Mom, I'm ready! I can do it, Mom! I'm going to fly on my own."...

You *are* ready to go, Teri. I assure you you *can* fly. It is time for you to do it. I don't think it was wrong for you to leave, I only wish you had chosen another way to do it....

You have mountains to climb – without me. I don't even know your world, I don't know your mountains.

You have my love. You have my support and my encouragement. (I cheer good.) You have me believing you can do what you *want* to do – whatever it is. That's all I can give you now. I've done the best I could do as your mother. I know I've failed you sometimes, it is unavoidable in raising a human being – especially when you are only a human being yourself, and you are still climbing your own mountains.

The best thing you can do is believe in yourself. Don't be afraid to try. Don't be afraid to fail.... Just dust yourself off and try again....

My love and thoughts go with you. My first child. My daughter.

Love, MOM.

JUDY GREEN HERBSTREIT, FROM A LETTER TO HER DAUGHTER, 1979

My Dear Mary,

How lonely the house seems – I never knew before how well you helped to fill it. I am anxious to hear of your first impressions of the city and how you like your new home. Ever since you went away, I have been wondering if it was as hard for you to go out into the world as it was for me to have you go.

Don't write short, hurried letters, simply stating facts in their tersest form, but tell me all your thoughts and dreams and plans, your worries and trials, and we will talk them over as two comrades.... If there is anything in my life that can be of value to you, I want you to have it; if I can save you a stumble or a single false step, I want to do it, but the only way I can do it is to know your heart.

Your loving mother

FLORENCE WENDEROTH SAUNDERS,
FROM "LETTERS TO A BUSINESS GIRL", 1908

One late afternoon I was waiting for a train on a country railway station. For some reason I found myself watching a woman come on to the platform. She was in her fifties, thick silver-grey hair, patterned sweater, trousers, an ordinary-looking, English, middle-aged woman....

Then I saw that the woman had come to see off her daughter. It was easy to tell she was her daughter because she had the same thick, though still brown, hair, the same pleasant-featured face with the same expression, and was even wearing an equivalent patterned sweater over her jeans. In fact she was a younger, slightly more up-to-date version of her mother. She was carrying a backpack.

The train came in. The daughter stepped into it. She leant out from the window so she could say goodbye to her mother, who stood nearby. Clearly, this was a long parting, no mere weekend break. They were very quiet in their farewells. They touched cheeks and their hands linked through the window. The train began to move slowly away. Their arms stretched and broke. The train moved faster. The girl stepped back from the window. The mother shook her head and turned briskly for the station exit.

The whole scene was so unsentimental, so unromantic, yet it was a lovers' parting.

RACHEL BILLINGTON, FROM "THE GREAT UMBILICAL"

Thirty-four years of unbroken kindness, of cloudless sunshine, of perpetual joy, of constant love. Thirty-four years of happy smiles, of loving looks and gentle words, of generous deeds. Thirty-four years, a flower, a palm, a star, a faultless child, a perfect woman, wife, and mother.

ROBERT G. INGERSOLL, IN A NOTE TO HIS DAUGHTER, EVA, ON HER BIRTHDAY

Daughters are more precious than gold.
More precious than any inanimate thing,
   however beautiful.
More precious than one's dreams, however
   glorious.
More precious than one's life.
They are your gift to the world.
They are its hope.
And yours to love.

MARION C. GARRETTY

Loveliness beyond completeness,
Sweetness distancing all sweetness,
Beauty all that beauty may be –
That's May Bennett, that's my baby.

WILLIAM COX BENNETT

My child is a Phenomenon, really the most
wonderful Natural Production I ever beheld....

LADY HOLLAND

Then farewell, my dear; my loved daughter,
    adieu;
The last pang of life is in parting from you.

THOMAS JEFFERSON

She is, I must confess, my most jealously-guarded obsession, and the late compelling spark in my life. I have spoilt her, no doubt, and overloaded her with expectations, most of which must have proved hard to bear.

But she has taught me more about women than I have learnt in a lifetime's devoted interest in the subject. The power to bruise and heal in one smooth-running sentence; to look blankly through you, then elect you king of the month. I have also had to learn to order, placate, encourage, disentangle and calm this one more than any other.

For in her I have watched the makings of a woman, year by year, almost day by day; from that plump breathing bundle first held in my arms to this assured beauty now standing shoulder to shoulder beside me.

LAURIE LEE, FROM "TWO WOMEN"

I have you fast in my fortress
    And will not let you depart,
But put you down into the dungeon
    In the round-tower of my heart.

And there will I keep you forever,
    Yes, forever and a day,
Till the wall shall crumble to ruin,
    And moulder in dust away.

HENRY WADSWORTH LONGFELLOW,
FROM "THE CHILDREN'S HOUR"

Acknowledgements: The publishers gratefully acknowledge permission to reprint copyright material. Whilst all reasonable efforts have been made to trace copyright holders and acknowledge sources and artists, the publishers would be pleased to hear from any copyright holders not here acknowledged.

RACHEL BILLINGTON, extracts from *The Great Umbilical,* published by Hutchinson. Reprinted by permission of David Higham Associates; JOHN CIARDI, "Someone's Face" from *I'm Mad At You!,* published in 1978 by William Collins; MARGARET DRABBLE, extract from *The Millstone,* published by Weidenfeld & Nicolson. Reprinted by permission of the Peters Fraser & Dunlop Group Ltd.; SALLY EMERSON, extract from "Back to Work" from *Occasional Poets,* published by Viking Penguin, 1986. © Sally Emerson 1986. Reprinted by permission of Sheil Land Associates; ROSE FYLEMAN, "Little Girl", from *Widdy-Widdy-Wurky, and Wanted,* published by Blackwell Publishers; JUDY GREEN HERBSTREIT, extract from *Between Ourselves,* edited by Karen Payne, first published by Michael Joseph; BRIAN JONES, extract from "You Being Born" from *Spitfire on the Northern Line* by Brian Jones, published by The Bodley Head. Reprinted by permission of Random House UK Ltd; LAURIE LEE, extracts from *Two Women,* © Laurie Lee 1983, first published by André Deutsch and by Penguin Books in 1984. Reprinted by permission of Penguin Books; SUE LIMB, extracts from *Love Forty,* published in 1988 by Corgi Books, a division of Transworld Publishers Ltd. Reprinted by permission of the Peters Fraser & Dunlop Group Ltd.; ANNE SEXTON, first stanza from "A Little Uncomplicated Hymn", from *Live or Die* by Anne Sexton. Copyright © 1966 by Anne Sexton. Reprinted by permission of Houghton Mifflin Company and Sterling Lord Literistic. All rights reserved.; MARGARET SLOAN-HUNTER, extract from "Passing" from *A Portrait of American Mothers & Daughters,* published by NewSage Press in 1987.; VIRGINIA WOOLF, extract from *A Writer's Diary,* published by Grafton Books, a division of HarperCollins Ltd, and Harcourt Brace Jovanovich Inc.

Picture Credits: Exley Publications is very grateful to the following individuals and organizations for permission to reproduce their pictures: Archiv Fur Kunst Und Geschichte (AKG), Art Resource (AR), The Bridgeman Art Library (BAL), Chris Beetle (CB), Christie's Colour Library (CCL), Edimedia (EDM), Fine Art Photographic Library Limited (FAP), Scala (S). Cover: MacGeorge, William "Sloe Blossom" (BAL); title page: Hacker, Arthur "In The Orchard" (BAL); page 6: Delacroix "Les Etatchez" (EDM); page 9: Hitz, Dora "Das Sonnenkind" (AKG); page 10: Farbdruck nach Gemalde von L.A. Tessier "Der Stammhalter" (AKG); page 13: Dorfh, Bertha "Portrait de bebe" (EDM); page 15: Pothast, Bernard "Dutch interior" (BAL); page 17: (CB); page 19: Sharp, Dorothea "Picking Flowers" (BAL); page 21: Larssoh "Le Repas Du Soir" (EDM); page 22: Meyerheim, F.E. "Family Chores" (CCL) ; pages 24-25 : Vallotton, Felix "The Balloon" (Giraudon/BAL); page 27: Bondzin, Gebhard "Annemone" (AKG); pages 28-29: © Erich Lessing. Gauguin, Paul "The Sleeping Child" (AR); pages 30-31: Kustodiev, Boris "La figlia dell artista alla finestra" (S); page 32: Renoir, Auguste "L'enfant au jouet" (EDM); page 34: Hughes, Arthur "L'enfant perdu" (CCL); page 36: McTaggart, William "Spring" (BAL); page 38: Larsson, Carl "Le cactus de Brita" (EDM); page 40: Bivel, Fernand "Au Coin du Jardin" (BAL); pages 42-43: Ditz "The Attic" (BAL); page 45: Renoir "Profile de jeune fille" (EDM); page 46: Bruford, Marjorie "In The Flower Fields" (BAL); page 49: Mucchi, Gabriele "Bildnis der Reisarbeiterin Ada" (AKG); page 51: Easton, Timothy "Autumn Grove" (BAL); page 53: Menzel, Adolph von "Das Balkonzimmer" (AKG); page 54: Kassatkin, Nikolai "Rivalinnen" (AKG); page 57: Edelfeldt, Albert "Ellan et Erik" (EDM); page 58: Finnie, John "A Morning On The Thames" (FAP); page 60: Friedrich, Caspar "Frau am Fenster" (AKG).